STORY WORDS

fancy   straight

squirted   modeling

fashion   jewelry

style

Total Word Count: 448

WHO ELSE IS SWIMMING IN THE OCEAN?

STONE ARCH READERS   LEVEL 3

THE BRAVE PUFFER FISH

STONE ARCH READERS   LEVEL 3

THE Hiding EEL

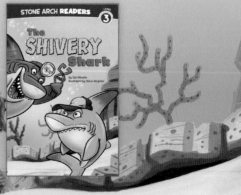

STONE ARCH READERS   LEVEL 3

The SHIVERY Shark

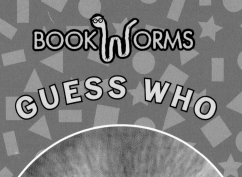

BOOK WORMS

GUESS WHO

Sniffs

Apple Jordan

mc **Marshall Cavendish**
Benchmark
New York

My nose is wet.

I can smell very well.

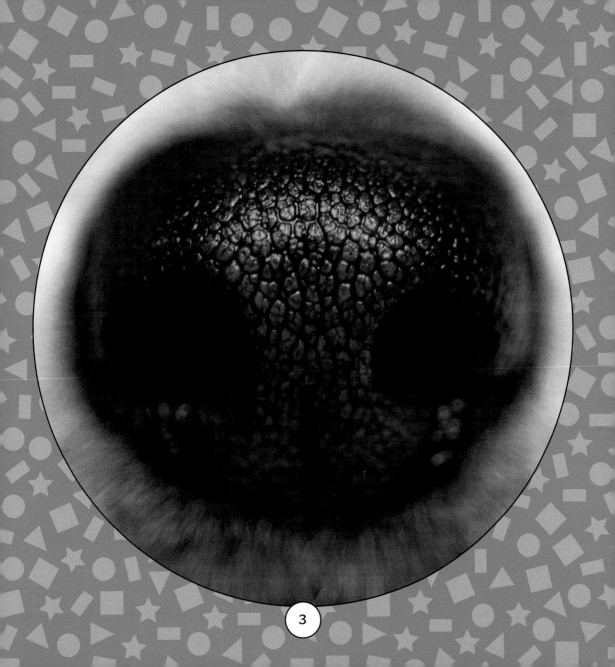

3

I have soft ears.

I can hear things
far away.

I have a shiny **coat**.

Sometimes I **shed**.

7

I like to run and jump.

I like to play.

I like to help.

I can lead the way.

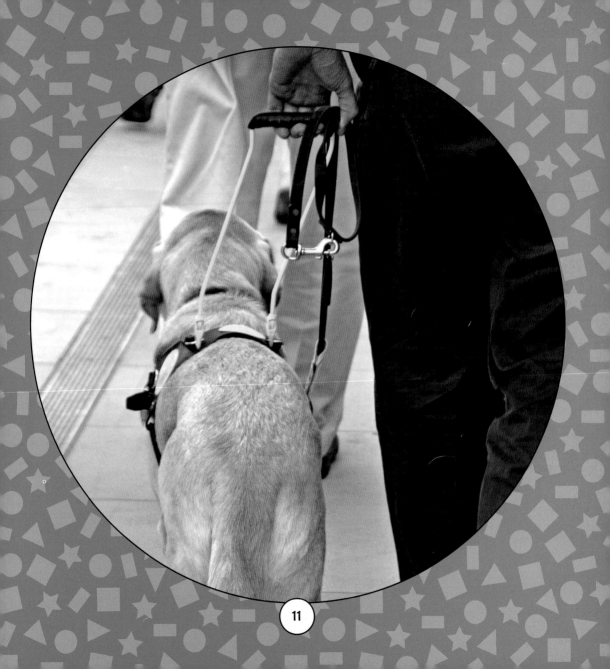

My babies are puppies.

They cannot see when they are born.

I bark when I am excited.

I growl if I am scared.

I wag my tail
when I am happy.

Who am I?

I am a dog!

Who Am I?

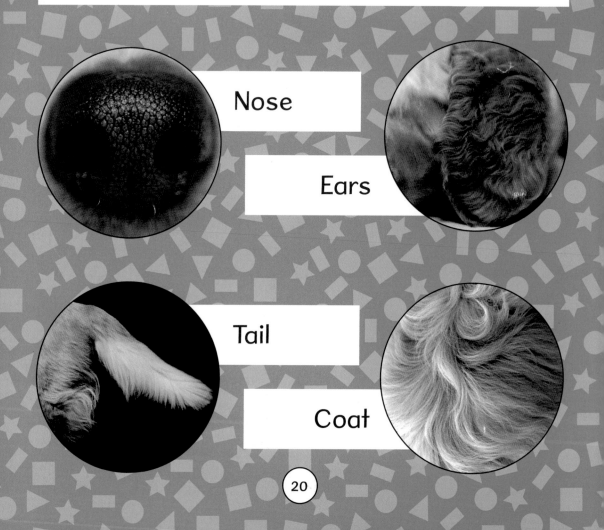

Nose

Ears

Tail

Coat

Puppies

Challenge Words

coat (kote) A dog's outer layer of fur.

shed (shed) To lose fur.

Index

Page numbers in **boldface** are illustrations.

About the Author

Apple Jordan has written many books for children, including a number of titles in the Bookworms series. She lives in upstate New York with her husband and two children. She volunteers at her local library and loves reading to kids.

With thanks to the Reading Consultants:

Nanci Vargas, Ed.D., is an Assistant Professor of Elementary Education at the University of Indianapolis.

Beth Walker Gambro is an Adjunct Profesor at the University of St. Francis in Joliet, Illinois.

Published by Marshall Cavendish Benchmark
An imprint of Marshall Cavendish Corporation

Other Marshall Cavendish Offices:
Marshall Cavendish International (Asia) Private Limited, 1 New Industrial Road, Singapore 536196 • Marshall Cavendish International (Thailand) Co Ltd. 253 Asoke, 12th Flr, Sukhumvit 21 Road, Klongtoey Nua, Wattana, Bangkok 10110, Thailand • Marshall Cavendish (Malaysia) Sdn Bhd, Times Subang, Lot 46, Subang Hi-Tech Industrial Park, Batu Tiga, 40000 Shah Alam, Selangor Darul Ehsan, Malaysia

Marshall Cavendish is a trademark of Times Publishing Limited

Library of Congress
Cataloging-in-Publication Data

Jordan, Apple.
Guess who sniffs / Apple Jordan.
p. cm. — (Guess who)
Includes index.
Summary: "Following a guessing game format, this book provides young readers with clues about a dog's physical characteristics, behaviors, and habitats, challenging readers to identify it"—Provided by publisher.
ISBN 978-1-60870-430-9
1. Dogs—Juvenile literature. I. Title.
SF426.5.J67 2012
636.7—dc22
2010039295

Editor: Joy Bean
Publisher: Michelle Bisson
Art Director: Anahid Hamparian
Series Designer: Virginia Pope

Photo research by Tracey Engel

Cover: Lisa A. Svara/Shutterstock
Title page: Pat Tuson/Alamy

The photographs in this book are used by permission and through the courtesy of: *Getty*: Daisuke Morita, 3, 20 (top, left); GK Hart/Vikki Hart, 17, 20 (bottom, left). *Alamy*: Gemstone Images, 5, 20 (top, right); mauritius images GmbH, 7, 20 (bottom, right); blickwinkel, 9; Pat Tuson, 11; Julian Pottage, 13, 21; Dan Sullivan, 15. *iStockphoto*: Mark Coffey, 19.

Printed in Malaysia (T)
1 3 5 6 4 2